GW00697267

This edition copyright © 2003 Lion Publishing
Illustrations copyright © 2003 Georgios Manoli

Published by
Lion Publishing plc
Mayfield House, 256 Banbury Road,
Oxford OX2 7DH, England
www.lion-publishing.co.uk
ISBN 0 7459 4666 6

First edition 2003
1 3 5 7 9 10 8 6 4 2 0

All rights reserved

Acknowledgments

9: 'Valentine', from *Serious Concerns* by Wendy Cope, copyright
© 1992 Wendy Cope, published by Faber and Faber Ltd. Used by
permission. 10, 24: 'The Examination' and 'Declaration of Intent',
from *Up To Date* by Steve Turner, copyright © 1993 Steve Turner,
published by Hodder and Stoughton Ltd. Used by permission. 13, 26:
Proverbs 30:18–19; Song of Songs 2:10–13, from the Good News
Bible published by The Bible Societies/HarperCollins Publishers Ltd,
UK © American Bible Society 1966, 1971, 1976, 1992, used with
permission. 16: 1 Corinthians 13:1–8, from the *Holy Bible, New
International Version*, copyright © 1973, 1978, 1984 by International
Bible Society. Used by permission. 20: 'A Song of Love (Sasha)' by
Else Lasker-Schüler, translated by Dalibor Warburton. 28: 'Come,
and Be My Baby', from *Complete Collected Poems* by Maya Angelou,
copyright © 1994 Maya Angelou, published by Virago Press by
arrangement with Random House Inc. Used by permission. 29: 'You
Come Too' by Rainer Maria Rilke, translated by M.D. Herter Norton.
Every effort has been made to trace and acknowledge copyright
holders of all the quotations in this book. We apologize for any errors
or omissions that may remain, and would ask those concerned to
contact the publishers, who will ensure that full acknowledgment
is made in the future.

A catalogue record for this book is available
from the British Library

Typeset in 10/15 Verdana
Printed and bound in Singapore

About Love

ILLUSTRATED BY
Georgios Manoli

LION
Giftlines

Celebration

Sonnet 18

Shall I compare thee to a summer's day?
Thou art more lovely and more temperate.
Rough winds do shake the darling buds of May,
And summer's lease hath all too short a date:
Sometime too hot the eye of heaven shines,
And often is his gold complexion dimmed;
And every fair from fair some time declines,
By chance, or nature's changing course, untrimmed;
But thy eternal summer shall not fade
Nor lose possession of that fair thou owest;
Nor shall death brag thou wanderest in his shade,
When in eternal lines to time thou growest.
So long as men can breathe or eyes can see,
So long lives this, and this gives life to thee.

William Shakespeare

A Red, Red Rose

O, my love's like a red, red rose,
That's newly sprung in June;
O, my love's like the melody
That's sweetly played in tune.

As fair art thou, my bonnie lass,
So deep in love am I:
And I will love thee still, my dear,
Till a' the seas gang dry.

Till a' the seas gang dry, my dear,
And the rocks melt wi' the sun;
I will love thee still, my dear,
While the sands o' life shall run.

And fare thee well, my only love,
And fare thee well awhile!
And I will come again, my love,
Though it were ten thousand mile!

Robert Burns

Valentine

My heart has made its mind up
And I'm afraid it's you.
Whatever you've got lined up,
My heart has made its mind up
And if you can't be signed up
This year, next year will do.
My heart has made its mind up
And I'm afraid it's you.

Wendy Cope

Recognition

The Examination

You set the first question
   you said
how much are you involved
   with me?
   and I
not being very good
   at science
said I didn't know.
I set the second question
   I said
how do you measure
   an emotion?
   and you
not being very good
   at languages
   smiled at me.

Steve Turner

I Do Not Love Thee...

I do not love thee! – no! I do not love thee!
And yet when thou art absent I am sad;
And envy even the bright blue sky above thee,
Whose quiet stars may see thee and be glad.

I do not love thee! – yet, I know not why,
Whate'er thou dost seems still well done, to me:
And often in my solitude I sigh
That those I do love are not more like thee!

I do not love thee! – yet, when thou art gone,
I hate the sound (though those who speak be dear)
Which breaks the lingering echo of the tone
Thy voice of music leaves upon my ear.

I do not love thee! – yet thy speaking eyes,
With their deep, bright, and most expressive blue,
Between me and the midnight heaven arise,
Oftener than any eyes I ever knew.

I know I do not love thee! yet, alas!
Others will scarcely trust my candid heart;
And oft I catch them smiling as they pass,
Because they see me gazing where thou art.

Caroline Elizabeth Sarah Norton

Four Things

There are four things that are
   too mysterious for me to understand:
an eagle flying in the sky,
a snake moving on a rock,
a ship finding its way over the sea,
and a man and a woman falling in love.

The Bible

Spelling It Out

Your Name

I wrote your name in the sand,
but the waves washed it away.
Then I wrote it in the sky,
but the wind blew it away.
So I wrote it in my heart,
and that's where it will stay.

Author unknown

Daydreaming

I find myself writing your name
over and over again

and I focus on our love
with every move of the pencil.

Ulrich Schaffer

Love Never Fails

If I speak in the tongues of men and of angels,
but have not love,
I am only a resounding gong or a clanging cymbal.
If I have the gift of prophecy
and can fathom all mysteries and all knowledge,
and if I have a faith that can move mountains,
but have not love, I am nothing.
If I give all I possess to the poor
and surrender my body to the flames,
but have not love, I gain nothing.
Love is patient, love is kind.
It does not envy, it does not boast, it is not proud.
It is not rude, it is not self-seeking,
it is not easily angered, it keeps no record of wrongs.
Love does not delight in evil
but rejoices with the truth.
It always protects, always trusts,
always hopes, always perseveres.
Love never fails.

The Bible

Sonnets from the Portuguese, XLIII

How do I love thee? Let me count the ways.
I love thee to the depth and breadth and height
My soul can reach, when feeling out of sight
For the ends of being and ideal grace.
I love thee to the level of every day's
Most quiet need, by sun and candlelight.
I love thee freely, as men strive for right;
I love thee purely, as they turn from praise.
I love thee with the passion put to use
In my old griefs, and with my childhood's faith.
I love thee with a love I seemed to lose
With my lost saints, – I love thee with the breath,
Smiles, tears, of all my life! – and, if God choose,
I shall but love thee better after death.

Elizabeth Barrett Browning

Longing

Sweet and Kind

There is a lady sweet and kind,
Was never a face so pleased my mind;
I did but see her passing by,
And yet I'll love her till I die.

Her gesture, motion, and her smiles,
Her wit, her voice, my heart beguiles,
Beguiles my heart, I know not why,
And yet I'll love her till I die.

Cupid is winged and he doth range
Her country, so, my love doth change:
But change she earth, or change she sky,
Yet, I will love her till I die.

Thomas Ford

A Song of Love (Sasha)

Ever since you left
The town has been dark.

I collect up the shadows
Of the palms
Under which you walked.

I must always hum a melody
That hangs smiling in the branches.

You love me again –
Who can I tell about my joy?

An orphan or a man on the way to a wedding,
Somebody to catch the echo of happiness.

I always know
When you think of me –

Because then my heart becomes a child
And cries.

At each entrance along the street
I stop and dream

And help the sun of your beauty to draw
On all the walls of the houses.

But I grow thin
Feeding on your picture.

Else Lasker-Schüler

Western Wind

Western wind, when wilt thou blow,
The small rain down can rain?
Christ, if my love were in my arms
And I in my bed again!

Anon (early sixteenth century)

Parting

Remember

Remember me when I am gone away,
Gone far away into the silent land;
When you can no more hold me by the hand,
Not I half turn to go yet turning stay.
Remember me when no more day by day
You tell me of our future that you planned:
Only remember me; you understand
It will be late to counsel then or pray.
Yet if you should forget me for a while
And afterwards remember, do not grieve:
For if the darkness and corruption leave
A vestige of the thoughts that once I had,
Better by far you should forget and smile
Than that you should remember and be sad.

Christina Rossetti

Declaration of Intent

She said she'd
love me for eternity
but reduced it
to eight months
for good behaviour.
She said we fitted
like a hand in a glove
but then the hot
weather came and such
accessories weren't needed.
She said the future
was ours but the deeds
were made out in
her name.
She said I was
the only one who
understood completely

and then she left me
and said she knew
that I'd understand completely.

Steve Turner

Love's Farewell

Since there's no help, come let us kiss and part,
Nay, I have done: you get no more of me,
And I am glad, yea, glad with all my heart,
That thus so cleanly I myself can free,
Shake hands for ever, cancel all our vows,
And when we meet at any time again,
Be it not seen in either of our brows
That we one jot of former love retain;
Now at the last gasp of love's latest breath,
When his pulse failing, passion speechless lies,
When faith is kneeling by his bed of death,
And innocence is closing up his eyes,
Now, if thou wouldst, when all have given him over,
From death to life thou might'st him yet recover.

Michael Drayton

Together

Come With Me

Come then, my love;
my darling, come with me.
The winter is over;
the rains have stopped;
in the countryside the flowers are in bloom.
This is the time for singing;
the song of doves is heard in the fields.
Figs are beginning to ripen;
the air is fragrant with blossoming vines.
Come then, my love;
my darling, come with me.

The Bible

Come, and Be My Baby

The highway is full of big cars
going nowhere fast
And folks is smoking anything that'll burn
Some people wrap their lives around a cocktail glass
And you sit wondering
where you're going to turn.
I got it.
Come. And be my baby.

Some prophets say the world is gonna end tomorrow
But others say we've got a week or two
The paper is full of every kind of blooming horror
And you sit wondering
what you're gonna do.
I got it.
Come. And be my baby.

Maya Angelou

You Come Too

Understand, I'll slip quietly
away from the noisy crowd
when I see the pale
stars rising, blooming, over the oaks.
I'll pursue solitary pathways
through the pale twilit meadows,
with only this one dream:
You come too.

Rainer Maria Rilke